COOKING FOR TWO

Sue Russell

Contents

This edition first published 1977 by
Octopus Books Limited
59 Grosvenor Street, London W1

Copyright©1977 Octopus Books Ltd

ISBN 0 7064 0644 3

Produced and printed in Hong Kong by
Mandarin Publishers Limited
22A Westlands Road, Quarry Bay

Photography: Norman Nicholls
Illustration: Michael Lodge

Frontispiece: Simple Cassoulet

PDO 77/379   1:2

Weights and Measures

Measurements are given in cups, tablespoons and teaspoons as well as pounds and ounces.

1 standard measuring cup 8 fl oz
1 standard measuring tablespoon 20 ml
1 standard measuring teaspoon 5 ml

All measurements given are level.
To level a cup measure of solid ingredients, shake the cup gently and check the measurements at eye level.
For an accurate spoon measure, level the ingredients off with the back of a palette, French or kitchen knife or with the back of a spatula.

Note   2½ cups liquid = 20 fl oz = 1 pint

Oven Temperature Guide

Description of Oven	Automatic Electric °F.	Gas °F.	Gas Regulo
Cool	200	200	0 – ½
Very Slow	250	250	½ – 1
Slow	300–325	300	1 – 2
Moderately Slow	325–350	325	2 – 3
Moderate	300–375	350	4
Moderately Hot	375–400	375	5
Hot	400–450	400	6 – 7
Very Hot	450–500	450	8 – 9

Introduction

Cooking for Two is a very personal and perhaps revolutionary cookbook. It sets out clearly and simply the easiest, most economical way in which to prepare and cook delicious and exciting food for those with little time for cooking, but who wish to ensure that there is always superb food served at their table for two! Many cookbooks provide painstaking methods of preparing food for those with lots of leisure hours, but just how many cookbooks are aimed at a busy career woman or housewife? Instead of dishing up dreary, precooked food you have rushed round to buy at your local supermarket or delicatessen just as it is closing, by reading this book and devoting a little thought and preplanning to purchasing the right ingredients, you can serve delicious meals seven days a week with little extra effort. Try to plan your shopping so that you buy once a week in bulk this cuts down on your valuable time, leaving you free to try out some of the chef-standard gourmet recipes in this book. Perhaps, once a week, choose a complete menu from your Cooking for Two, set the table with your best cutlery and linen, decorate it up with flowers and candles, put on your prettiest dress, and wait for your man's surprise and delight when you serve up a fabulous meal. It will pay off dividends!

There is an exciting range of completely new Breakfast recipes you've never even dreamed of for intimate breakfasts. Or try out a breakfast party on your friends (just up the quantities per couple) served with Morning Glory — champagne and orange juice. Buy the cheapest champagne at your liquor store and add fresh-squeezed orange juice in equal quantities.

The hors d'oeuvre or Starters and Soups provide an exciting introduction to the Main Courses. These recipes, carefully planned for nourishment and eye appeal, some completely new, others traditional favourites, are all chosen for ease of preparation and their superb flavour. Delicate or filling Desserts round off the meal.

Many of the recipes contained in this book are ideal for cooking ahead, the day or night before. They can be stored in your refrigerator until ready for garnishing, heating and serving. The Salads and Vegetable recipes provide an ideal accompaniment to the meat, poultry and fish recipes of the Main Courses; some of them are meals in themselves. Try out some of the unique Salad recipes at your next barbecue or picnic.

Essentially this is a book for two people with quantities carefully chosen to avoid wastage, and to ensure that you, in your busy life, and with the minimum of fuss are a superb cook.

The publishers sincerely thank the following for their assistance in compiling this book:

Norman Nicholls, Jean Wright, Anne Marshall, The Bay Tree Pty. Ltd. and Incorporated Agencies Pty. Ltd.

Eggs en Cocotte

Breakfasts

Eggs en Cocotte

Oven temperature: 350-375°, Gas Mark 4-5

Cooking time: 8-10 minutes

butter for greasing
salt
pepper
2-4 eggs
¼ oz (approx. 1 teaspoon) melted butter per egg
1 teaspoon cream per egg

Grease individual ovenproof cocotte dishes, 1 egg to a very
small dish, or use a larger dish which will hold 2 eggs, or one
good-sized ovenproof dish which will hold 4 eggs. Grease
dishes liberally with butter and sprinkle with salt and pepper.
Break eggs into dishes. Pour melted butter and cream over the
top. Stand dishes in a baking dish of hot water and place in a
moderate oven for 8-10 minutes.
Eggs continue cooking after the dishes are removed from the
oven, so do not overcook.
Variation: Before putting eggs into greased dishes, put in 2
teaspoons of chopped ham or lightly sauteed mushrooms
per egg.

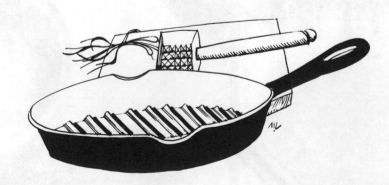

10

Continental Breakfast

Oven temperature: 350-375°, Gas Mark 4-5

Cooking time: 5-7 minutes

strong, black, freshly percolated coffee
bread rolls, preferably the knotted ones sprinkled with poppy
    or sesame seeds
orange or grapefruit juice, freshly squeezed
½ pint milk
butter
jam
mild cheeses
cooked ham, thinly sliced
2 apples and 2 oranges

Percolate coffee, using 4 tablespoons medium ground coffee
and 1 pint freshly drawn cold water.
Dampen rolls with milk, or use frozen bread rolls. Place the
rolls in a moderate oven for 5-7 minutes.
Serve juice.
Heat milk until almost boiling, bring to the table with coffee
in a separate jug.
Serve hot rolls with butter, jam, cheeses (such as Bel Paese,
Edam, Gouda) and sliced ham, rolled up and secured with
toothpicks.
Fresh apples and oranges can be served, whether eaten or not,
they look fresh and bright on the breakfast table.
Pour half milk, half coffee into big breakfast mugs or, if
preferred, serve black coffee made according to taste.
You may like to add a boiled or poached egg to this breakfast.

Soufflé Omelette

Cooking time: 5 minutes

4 eggs, separated
1 tablespoon castor sugar
1 tablespoon cream
1 oz butter
1 tablespoon strawberry jam
½ punnet strawberries, sliced
extra castor sugar for serving

Beat egg yolks in a mixing bowl with sugar and cream. Whisk egg whites until firm and fold into egg yolk misture.
Heat omelette pan, add butter and when butter is sizzling pour in the egg mixture. Allow to cook over a low to moderate heat until just set (1-1½ minutes), then brown under a medium — hot grill.
Spread with jam and sliced strawberries and fold over. Slide from pan, sprinkle with sugar and serve immediately.
This omelette is delicious when served for a late breakfast or brunch.

Scrambled Eggs

Cooking time: 10 minutes

1 oz butter
4 eggs
salt and pepper
a little chopped parsley

Melt half the butter in a saucepan (preferably a non-stick pan) and add the eggs which have been well beaten and seasoned with salt and pepper.
Cook over a low heat, until eggs start to thicken, add the rest of the butter and keep stirring for another 30 seconds, then remove from heat. Stir in chopped parsley.
Serve at once on hot buttered toast.

Boiled Eggs

Cooking time: 3-5 minutes

1 or 2 eggs per person

Bring a small saucepan of water to the boil; add a teaspoon of salt and a tablespoon of vinegar as this will stop the white from escaping if the egg shells crack.
Do not use eggs straight from the refrigerator as these will crack if plunged directly into boiling water.
Take eggs at room temperature and gently lower on a large spoon into the boiling water.
Allow eggs to simmer gently for 3-5 minutes according to taste.
Remove from pan and serve immediately with salt and pepper and fingers of hot buttered toast.

French Omelette

Cooking time: 2 minutes

4 eggs
1 tablespoon cold water
1 teaspoon salt
freshly ground black pepper
1½ oz butter

Break eggs into a basin and beat thoroughly with a fork. Add water, salt and pepper and mix together.
Heat omelette pan over medium heat and add butter. When butter is sizzling, pour in egg mixture. After about 15 seconds gently stir twice round the pan with the back of a fork.
Leave to set again for a few seconds, then, using a palette knife, loosen omelette from one side and fold about a third over then loosen and fold a third over from the other side.
Turn pan over and slip omelette onto a warm plate and serve at once.
An omelette pan should be heavy-based and have rounded edges. An 8-inch diameter pan will hold four eggs, sufficient

for breakfast for two. If possible the pan should be kept for omelettes (and pancakes) only and not washed with soap but merely wiped out with some absorbent kitchen paper or a clean cloth.

Variation: Tomato omelette: Cut 2 medium size tomatoes into ¼-inch slices. Sauté lightly in 1 oz butter and sprinkle with salt and pepper. Place across centre of omelette as it is just cooked, then fold over as for basic omelette. Serve sprinkled with finely chopped parsley.

Grills

Grilled bacon, lambs' kidneys, baby lamb loin chops, sausages and tomato, in various combinations, make a sustaining and appetising breakfast.
Suitable portions for each person are two small lean chops and half a tomato, or one lamb kidney, one rasher of bacon and half a tomato, but you may decide on the quantity and variety according to your appetite.
To grill, preheat the grill at highest heat for 5 minutes before starting to cook, so that meats are sealed quickly and juices retained.
Chops should be trimmed of excess fat, grilled quickly for 1 minute on each side to seal in the juices, then sprinkled with salt and pepper and returned to cook under a low-medium heat for a further 5-10 minutes or until cooked.
Lambs' kidneys should be skinned, cut in two lengthwise, the fatty core and tubes removed with kitchen scissors, then grilled, first on the cut side, then on the other, for 3-4 minutes on each side.
Sausages should be well-pricked and, depending on size, may need to be cooked for as long as 15-20 minutes, turning regularly.
Tomatoes should be cut in half, across centre, not through stalk, and placed under a hot grill for about 5 minutes.
Bacon rashers cook in 3-5 minutes under a hot grill and should be turned just once. Drain before serving. Serve all grilled breakfasts immediately they are cooked.

Fried Eggs and Candied Cooked Ham

Oven temperature: 375-400°, Gas Mark 5-6

Cooking time: 15 minutes

½ oz butter
2 tablespoons pineapple juice
2 slices cooked ham, ¼-inch thick
1 tablespoon brown sugar
1 or 2 eggs per person

Melt butter in an ovenproof dish. Add pineapple juice. Put
ham slices in dish and sprinkle with brown sugar. Put into a
moderately hot oven to heat for 10 minutes.
When ham is almost ready, heat frying pan containing ¼-inch
vegetable oil until oil sizzles when a drop of water is flicked
into it.
Break eggs gently into oil, keeping them apart if possible.
Baste them while they cook by spooning hot oil over until a
film of white is set over the egg yolk. Lift eggs from oil with
an egg slice and drain well. Serve with hot candied ham.
Variation: Serve eggs with fried bacon; cut rind from bacon
and fry bacon in a heated, greased frying pan over a medium
heat, turn once and cook until well-browned but still moist.
Keep ham warm while frying eggs.

Fried eggs and candied cooked ham

First Courses

Chicken Liver Pâté

Cooking time: 5 minutes

8 oz chicken livers
2 oz butter
1 tablespoon sherry or brandy
1 clove garlic, chopped and crushed
pinch of dried thyme
pinch of mixed spice
salt
freshly ground black pepper
extra melted butter

Clean the chicken livers well, removing any membrane or tubes.
Sauté chicken livers gently in half the butter for 3 minutes; they should still be pink inside. Remove the livers and add the sherry or brandy to the pan.
Mash the livers well with a wooden spoon, add the garlic, the rest of the butter (melted), thyme, mixed spice and a little salt and pepper.
Stir in the liquor from the pan and spoon the pâté into a small earthenware bowl. Pour some extra melted butter over to cover the top to seal in the flavour. Chill well.
Serve with hot toast.
This makes more than enough for two, but keeps well in the refrigerator for a day or two.

Aubergine Dip

Preparation time: 15 minutes

1 medium size aubergine
1 clove garlic, crushed
salt
freshly ground black pepper
olive oil
1 teaspoon lemon juice
1 tablespoon finely chopped parsley
rye bread for serving

This can be served as an appetiser, entrée or as part of a salad.
Cut the aubergine in half lengthwise.
Grill the aubergine until it is soft throughout. Scoop out the
flesh and mash it in a dish with a wooden spoon. Mix in the
garlic and salt and pepper to taste.
Add very slowly some olive oil until you have a thickish
purée, then stir in the lemon juice and chopped parsley.
Serve with slices of rye bread.

Oeufs en Gelée

Cooking time: 5 minutes

2 eggs
1 thick slice cooked ham
1 medium size can consommé
2 teaspoons sherry
chopped tarragon

Carefully poach the eggs in boiling, salted water to which you
have added a dash of vinegar or lemon juice, take them out
before the yolks are set — they should be rather runny. To
stop them cooking beyond the desired point, add cold water
to the pan in which they are cooking, then remove them.
Divide the ham between two cocottes or small individual
dishes and carefully place a poached egg in each, being very
careful not to break the yolk.
Cover with enough consommé, to which you have added the
sherry, to just cover the eggs.
Sprinkle with a little chopped tarragon and chill.
Serve in the cocottes.

Mushrooms Vinaigrette

Preparation time: 10 minutes

4 oz fresh mushrooms
3 tablespoons olive oil
1 tablespoon lemon juice
1 clove garlic, crushed
salt and freshly ground black pepper
1 teaspoon finely chopped parsley

Wipe mushrooms with a clean, damp cloth and slice thinly;
do not remove the stalks.
Combine oil, lemon juice, garlic, salt, pepper and parsley.
Pour the dressing over the mushrooms and make sure they
are coated on all sides.
Chill, covered, for several hours before serving. The raw
mushrooms are extremely absorbent so you may have to
put some more of the dressing on them.
Serve chilled.

Egg and Cheese Soup

Cooking time: 8 minutes

1 pint chicken stock, made with stock cubes
1 egg yolk
1 tablespoon finely grated cheese

Heat the stock to boiling point.
Beat the egg yolk well with the grated cheese.
Pour about half the stock into the egg yolk mixture slowly,
return to the pan with the rest of the stock and bring almost
to the boil, stirring continuously.
Serve hot.

Sautéed Prawns

Cooking time: 10 minutes

butter for sauteeing
8 king prawns, unshelled
salt
freshly ground black pepper
chopped fresh parsley and fennel
lemon juice
French bread for serving

Melt enough butter in a small heavy frying pan to cover the
bottom of the pan well. When the butter is bubbling, add the
prawns in their shells. Cook gently for about 5 minutes on
each side until they are pink.
Remove pan from heat, shell the prawns, but leave on the
tails. Season to taste with salt and pepper, a little parsley and
fennel and lemon juice.
Serve hot with crusty French bread.

Egg and Lemon Soup

Cooking time: 20 minutes

1 pint chicken stock, made with stock cubes
salt and pepper
1 tablespoon uncooked rice
1 egg
juice of 1 lemon, strained
chopped parsley for garnish

Bring the stock to the boil, season to taste with salt and
pepper.
Add rice to the boiling stock and simmer until tender,
covered, for about 12 minutes.
As the soup cooks, beat the egg in a mixing bowl then
gradually beat in the lemon juice and very slowly add 2/5 of
the boiling stock.
Add this mixture to the soup while it is still cooking, stirring
all the time.
Simmer gently for 3 minutes and remove from heat.
Allow to stand for 2 minutes before serving sprinkled with
chopped parsley.

Moules Marinière

Cooking time: 5-10 minutes

3 pints mussels
5 tablespoons dry white wine or cider
1 small onion, chopped
1 clove garlic, chopped
½ stalk celery, sliced
a handful of chopped parsley

Make sure your mussels come from a reliable source, i.e. from
unpolluted water, as mussels (like oysters) tend to collect
any impurities present in the water.
Discard any mussels that have holes in them or are open.
Remove the beards with a knife and scrape off any marine
growth such as barnacles or small shells which may be
adhering to the shells. Scrub them well and wash in plenty of
cold water until the water is clean and free of grit.
Place washed mussels in a wide pan with wine, onion, garlic,
celery and parsley and cook over a high heat until the shells
open. Remove from the heat the minute the shells open.
Serve immediately in two warmed tureens or casseroles with
the cooking liquid poured over them. It is a good idea to
provide another plate for the empty shells.

Prawns in Cream Sauce

Cooking time: 10 minutes

6 oz prawns, cooked and shelled
freshly ground black pepper
pinch of ground nutmeg
1½ oz butter
1 tablespoon brandy
¼ pint thick cream
1 teaspoon finely chopped parsley
boiled rice and lemon wedges for serving

Season the prawns with pepper and nutmeg.
Heat the butter in a small frying pan and sauté the prawns
over a gentle heat for 3 minutes.
Flame the prawns with brandy (warm brandy gently in a
large spoon or ladle, ignite and pour flaming brandy into the
pan). When the flames have gone out, reduce heat to low and
cook for a further 2 minutes. Increase the heat and add the
cream. Cook until the cream thickens, shake the pan and stir
the sauce. Stir in the parsley.
Serve hot on boiled rice, garnished with lemon wedges.

Stuffed Avocado Pears

Preparation time: 5 minutes

1 avocado pear
1 teaspoon white wine vinegar
1 anchovy, finely chopped
½ teaspoon paprika
2 tablespoons cream
salt and pepper
lemon wedges for serving

Cut the avocado in half lengthwise and remove the stone.
Scoop out the avocado flesh and mash well with a wooden
spoon.
Add the vinegar, chopped anchovy, paprika and cream to the
mashed avocado flesh and mix well. Season to taste with salt
and pepper.
Pile mixture into the empty shells and serve chilled, garnished
with lemon wedges.

Prawns in cream sauce

Escargots Bourguignonne

Oven temperature: 375-400°, Gas Mark 5-6

Cooking time: 8 minutes

2 dozen canned snails
5 tablespoons finely chopped parsley
1 shallot, finely chopped
1 clove garlic, chopped and pounded
4 oz unsalted butter
freshly ground black pepper
salt

You will need specially designed dishes to cook your snails in. These are circular and have an indentation to hold each in its shell.
Alternatively, you can use the little snail pots called 'godets', which are very much like an egg cup and hold one snail each. They dispense with the necessity for special eating utensils and are also less likely to tip over on the way from the oven to the table.
Drain snails well. Mix together the parsley, shallot and garlic. Work this into the unsalted butter and season with pepper and the smallest pinch of salt (tinned snails are usually quite salty).
Put a little knob of the flavoured butter into each shell (or godet), add the snail, press it in quite firmly and then add more butter so that the shell is as full as possible.
Put the filled shells, open end up, in special snail pans, cover with aluminium foil and cook in a moderately hot oven for about 8 minutes. Be very careful not to let the snails tip over as all the garlic butter will spill out.
Serve hot with hot garlic bread.

Chick Pea Soup

Cooking time: 1½ hours

4 oz chick peas, soaked overnight*
½ onion, sliced
1 clove garlic, crushed
1 anchovy fillet, chopped
½ green pepper, seeded, cored and chopped
2 tablespoons olive oil
2 tomatoes, skinned and chopped
pinch of dried rosemary
salt and pepper
2 oz small noodles

Put the soaked chick peas in a pan with 2 pints of cold water
and bring to the boil. Simmer gently until peas are tender but
not mushy. Strain and retain cooking liquor.
Fry the onion, garlic, anchovy and green pepper in olive oil in
a frying pan until tender but not browned.
Add the tomatoes and rosemary and simmer gently for about
10 minutes.
Add the vegetable mixture to the chick peas and ½ pint of
the liquid they have been cooking in.
Add salt and pepper to taste and bring to the boil.
Add the noodles and continue simmering until tender.
Serve hot.
*Note: Haricot beans or lentils may be used in place of chick
peas in this recipe.

French Onion Soup

Cooking time: 30 minutes

1 oz butter
1 large onion, thinly sliced
2 teaspoons plain flour
¾ pint beef stock, made with stock cube
1 teaspoon sugar
salt
freshly ground black pepper
French bread
grated cheese

Heat the butter in a heavy-based pan, add the onion and
cook, stirring continuously, until the onion is soft and golden.
Do not overcook.
Stir in the flour for 1 minute then slowly stir in the stock.
Add the sugar. Season to taste with salt and pepper.
Cover and simmer gently for 20 minutes.
Toast some slices of French bread and sprinkle generously
with grated cheese. Grill until cheese melts and bubbles.
Top each bowl of soup with a slice of cheese-topped toast
and serve hot.

French onion soup

Iced Cucumber Soup

Preparation time: 10 minutes

½ fresh cucumber
1 x 8 oz carton plain yoghurt
6 tablespoons iced water
2 cloves garlic, 1 crushed and 1 chopped finely and crushed
3 teaspoons olive oil
1 teaspoon chopped mint
2 tablespoons sultanas, plumped in hot water
salt

Peel and dice the cucumber and sprinkle with salt.
Beat the yoghurt until smooth in a mixing bowl and stir in the iced water.
Drain the cucumber and dry with a clean tea towel.
Rub another bowl with the crushed garlic.
Place the oil in this bowl and stir in the yoghurt and water, cucumber, mint, sultanas and chopped and crushed garlic.
Chill before serving.

Vichyssoise

Cooking time: 20-30 minutes

8 oz leeks, peeled and sliced
1 large potato, peeled and sliced
½ onion, sliced
4 sprigs parsley, tied together
½ pint chicken stock, made from a stock cube
½ pint milk
salt
white pepper
chopped chives for garnish

Put the vegetables in a saucepan with the parsley and pour in the stock. Cover and cook gently until all the vegetables are tender.
Discard the parsley and sieve the vegetables. This will be a little difficult, so moisten them with a little of the milk.
Gradually add more milk until the soup is the consistency of thin cream, then season to taste with salt and pepper.
Serve soup either hot or chilled.
Garnish with chopped chives.

Gazpacho

Preparation time: 14 minutes

1 large ripe tomato
¼ cucumber
¼ green pepper, seeded and cored
3 shallots
2 teaspoons olive oil
1 teaspoon white wine vinegar
5 tablespoons chilled water
1 clove garlic, crushed
salt and pepper
ice cubes

A refreshing summer soup.
Skin tomato by plunging into boiling water then removing skin.
Purée the tomato in an electric blender or press through a sieve.
Peel and finely dice the cucumber.
Dice green pepper finely.
Thinly slice the shallots.
Stir the prepared vegetables into the tomato purée along with the oil, vinegar and chilled water. Add the garlic and season to taste with salt and pepper.
Chill soup well before serving.
Serve with an ice cube in each bowl.

Courgettes à la Grecque

Cooking time: 30 minutes

1 lb small courgettes
4 tablespoons olive oil
juice of 1 lemon
½ pint water
1 bay leaf
2 pinches chopped thyme
6 crushed peppercorns
¼ teaspoon coriander seeds
2 tomatoes, skinned and chopped
1 clove garlic, crushed
salt

Wash the courgettes and cut off any damaged skin. Remove
both ends and slice into 1 inch pieces. Place in a colander and
sprinkle with salt. Leave for one hour to drain.
Bring the oil, lemon juice, water, bay leaf, thyme,
peppercorns and coriander seeds to the boil in a saucepan.
Add the tomatoes and courgettes, previously dried with a
clean tea towel. Cook quite fast for 20 minutes, uncovered.
Drain off any remaining water. Add the garlic, sprinkle with
salt and chill before serving.

Stuffed Peaches

Preparation time: 8-10 minutes

3 oz cream cheese
1 tablespoon sultanas (plumped in boiling water beforehand)
1 tablespoon chopped walnuts
1 large unblemished ripe peach or two halves of canned peach
2 crisp lettuce leaves.

Mix the cheese, sultanas and nuts and make into about 6
small balls. If these balls are very soft, chill the mixture in the
refrigerator for a short time.
Arrange the peach halves on a lettuce leaf in two individual
bowls or glasses and place three cheese balls into each. Serve
chilled.

Main Courses

Cold Marinated Salmon

Cooking time: 30 minutes

1 lb salmon (or turbot) in two slices or steaks
plain flour for coating
¼ pint olive oil
1 small carrot, peeled and thinly sliced
1 small onion, thinly sliced
1 tablespoon finely chopped parsley
salt
6 peppercorns
1 little mustard
1 bay leaf
¼ pint white wine
¼ pint white vinegar
juice of ¼ lemon

Lightly coat the fish with plain flour and fry in olive oil on
both sides until golden brown. Drain well.
Put the fish aside in a small earthenware dish.
Fry the sliced carrot and onion and chopped parsley lightly
in the oil in which you fried the fish.
Add a pinch of salt, the peppercorns, mustard to taste, bay
leaf, wine, vinegar and lemon juice.
Bring to the boil and simmer for 10 minutes.
Pour over the fish and chill for at least a day before serving.
Serve with salad.

Trout with Almonds

Cooking time: 15 minutes

2 cleaned trout, about 10 inches long
salt
freshly ground black pepper
plain flour for coating
4 oz butter
1 teaspoon lemon juice, strained
2 oz almonds, toasted
chopped parsley
lemon slices

Sprinkle the trout, both inside and out with salt and pepper
and toss lightly in flour.
Heat half the butter in a heavy-based frying pan and fry the
fish until well browned on both sides. Put aside and keep
warm.
Add the rest of the butter to the pan with the lemon juice,
more pepper and toasted almonds, simmer for a few minutes
and pour over the fish.
Garnish with chopped parsley and lemon wedges and serve
piping hot.

Herring Salad

Preparation time: 15 minutes.

2 salted herrings
milk and water
olive oil
white wine vinegar
1 hard-boiled egg, chopped
capers for garnish

Soak the herrings overnight in half milk and water to cover.
Drain and dress with oil and vinegar to cover. Sprinkle with
egg and garnish with a few capers.
Serve chilled with salad.

Cold Fish in White Wine

Cooking time: 20 minutes

2 mackerel, herring or mullet
½ pint dry white wine or cider
¾ pint water
1 onion, sliced
a little fennel
strip of lemon peel
4 whole peppercorns
1 bay leaf
salt
French mustard
chopped parsley

Clean the fish, remove fins and tail.
Simmer wine or cider, water, onion, a little fennel, lemon
peel, peppercorns, bay leaf and a pinch of salt together for
10 minutes, strain and leave the liquid to cool.
Poach the cleaned fish in this bouillon as gently as possible
for about 10 minutes or until the fish is no longer pink in the
middle.
Carefully lift the fish from the liquid and remove all skin.
Divide each fish into two fillets and remove bones.
Strain off ¾ pint of the liquid and stir in a little French
mustard to taste.
Pour this over the fish and garnish with chopped parsley.
Chill before serving. Serve with cucumber salad.

Sole Véronique

Oven temperature: 350-375°F, Gas Mark 4-5

Cooking time: 30 minutes

2 fillets of sole, skinned
½ small onion, sliced
1 bay leaf
4 peppercorns
2 teaspoons lemon juice, strained
1 oz butter
1 tablespoon plain flour
½ pint milk
salt and pepper
small bunch green grapes, peeled

Roll up the fillets of sole, skinned side inside, and secure with
a toothpick.
Stand upright in a greased ovenproof dish with sliced onion,
bay leaf, peppercorns and lemon juice. Add enough water
to half cover the fish.
Cover and cook in a moderate oven until tender, about
25-30 minutes.
Put fish aside and keep hot, reserving ¼ pint of the liquid.
Melt butter in a small saucepan, stir in the flour and cook for
1 minute. Remove from heat and slowly add the milk and the
reserved liquid, which has been reduced by fast boiling to
half its original quantity.
Return to heat; bring to the boil, stirring continuously and
simmer until smooth and thick.
Season to taste with salt and pepper.
To serve, pour sauce over fish and surround with grapes.

Mediterranean Fish Stew

Cooking time: 30 minutes

1 firm-fleshed fish, about 12 oz — mullet, herring, mackerel
   or plaice
1 large onion, sliced
1 clove garlic, crushed
olive oil for frying
1 x 15 oz can tomatoes
1 tablespoon white wine
3 tablespoons chopped parsley
1 lemon
boiled rice for serving
parsley sprigs for garnish

Clean the fish and remove the head, fins and tail. Cut fish
into 2-inch pieces.
Fry the fish, onion and garlic lightly in a little olive oil.
Add the tomatoes with their juice, wine, chopped parsley and
half the lemon cut in slices, cover and simmer slowly until
the fish is tender, about 15-20 minutes.
Remove any bones and the remains of the lemon slices.
Serve fish stew on a bed of hot boiled white rice, garnished
with parsley sprigs and the remaining ½ lemon, cut into
wedges.
Serve hot with a spoon and fork.

Pepper Steak

Cooking time: 8-15 minutes

2 slices fillet or rump steak, 4-8 oz each
3 teaspoons whole black peppercorns
2 oz butter
1 tablespoon olive oil
2 teaspoons brandy
1 teaspoon butter

Trim steaks neatly and beat with a rolling pin.
Crush the peppercorns coarsely with a rolling pin. Press these
into the steaks on both sides and allow to stand for about
1 hour.
Heat butter and oil in a heavy-based frying pan and cook the
steaks quickly on both sides to seal in the juices. Complete
cooking according to taste — rare, medium or well-done.
Remove from pan and keep hot.
Stir in the brandy into the pan juices and bring to the boil,
scraping the sediment from the pan. Remove from heat and
stir in the extra butter. Pour this sauce over the steaks and
serve immediately with vegetables or tossed green salad.

Pepper Steak

Steak Diane

Cooking time: 5 minutes

12 oz fillet steak, 1 inch thick
freshly ground black pepper
3 oz butter
1 clove garlic, crushed
1 tablespoon Worcestershire sauce
1 tablespoon chopped parsley
1 tablespoon cream

The steak should be bought 1 inch thick and then pounded
until very thin with a meat cleaver, mallet or rolling pin.
Cut into two equal pieces.
Lightly season the steaks on both sides with the pepper.
Put butter in a heavy-based frying pan and when sizzling add
the steaks.
While the steaks are cooking on one side, rub garlic into the
top of them with a wooden spoon.
Turn the steak over and add the Worcestershire sauce to the
pan, moving the steak around in the juices.
When cooked to taste, transfer to a hot serving plate and
sprinkle with chopped parsley. Stir the cream into the pan
juices, heat thoroughly and pour the sauce over the steak.
Serve immediately with tossed green salad.

Carpetbag Steak

Cooking time: 8-15 minutes

1 lb lean rump or fillet steak, about 3 inches thick
salt and pepper
1 bottle (1 dozen) oysters
butter for frying
1 oz butter for serving

Cut the steak into two pieces.
Make a pocket in each piece of steak with a very sharp, pointed knife.
Season the pocket with salt and pepper and stuff half the drained oysters into each pocket.
Fasten the pockets with small skewers or wooden toothpicks.
Pan fry the steaks in butter in a heavy-based frying pan.
Serve immediately, dotted with extra butter, accompanied with freshly cooked vegetables or tossed green salad.

Goulash

Cooking time: 1¾ hours

1 lb stewing beef or veal
1 large onion, sliced
2 tablespoons oil
1 tablespoon paprika
1 small can tomato purée
salt
potatoes, rice or noodles for serving
sour cream or yoghurt for serving

Trim the meat carefully and cut into 2 inch pieces.
Fry meat and onions in heated oil in a heavy-based saucepan or flame-proof casserole until the meat is slightly browned and the onions are transparent.
Add paprika, tomato purée and enough cold water to cover.
Stir well, add salt to taste, cover and simmer gently until the meat is tender, about 1½ hours.
Serve hot with plain boiled potatoes, rice or noodles, topped with a spoonful of sour cream or yoghurt.

Spaghetti Etcetera

Cooking time: 20 minutes

4 oz spaghetti
3 tablespoons olive oil
8 oz fresh mushrooms, wiped and sliced
2 onions, thinly sliced
2 cloves garlic, crushed
5 anchovy fillets, chopped
3 rashers lean bacon, rinded and chopped
6 black olives
a handful of fresh parsley, roughly chopped
grated Parmesan cheese for serving

Cook the spaghetti in a large saucepan of boiling, salted water
until tender, about 15-20 minutes.
Meanwhile, heat the oil in a heavy-based pan and gently cook,
covered, the mushrooms, onions, garlic, anchovy fillets,
bacon, olives and parsley for about 15 minutes.
Serve the hot, drained spaghetti topped with the savoury
mixture and grated Parmesan cheese.

Chilli Con Carne

Cooking time: 1¾ hours

2 tablespoons oil
1 onion, chopped
1 clove garlic, crushed
12 oz best quality minced beef
1 x 5 oz can tomato purée
3 dried red chillis or 2 teaspoons chilli powder
1 bay leaf
pinch of thyme
salt and pepper
1 x 10 oz can red kidney beans

Heat oil in heavy-based saucepan, add chopped onion and garlic and cook until soft.
Add the meat and cook until the meat changes colour, stirring frequently.
Stir in the tomato purée, dried chillis or chilli powder and sufficient cold water to cover the meat.
Add bay leaf and thyme and season to taste with salt and pepper.
Simmer gently, uncovered, stirring frequently, for about an hour, and add a little water if the sauce reduces too much.
Add the drained kidney beans and simmer for a further 30 minutes; keep the juice from the beans and add a little of this if the chilli con carne becomes dry.
This dish improves if it is cooked the day before and reheated.
Serve hot with boiled rice.

Spaghetti Bolognese

Cooking time: 45 minutes

2 tablespoons olive oil
1 small onion, chopped
1 clove garlic, crushed
12 oz best quality minced beef
2 oz mushrooms, wiped and sliced
4 tablespoons red wine
1 x 5 oz can tomato purée
pinch of dried basil
1 lump or 1 teaspoon sugar
1 bay leaf
cold water or stock, made with stock cube
4 oz spaghetti
grated Parmesan cheese for serving

In a heavy-based pan, heat the oil and fry the onion and
garlic until soft. Add the meat and mushrooms and cook
until the meat changes colour.
Add the wine and allow this to bubble until reduced by half,
stirring the meat all the time with a wooden spoon. Add the
tomato purée, basil, sugar, bay leaf and enough stock or
water to give a thin consistency as the sauce will reduce
considerably with cooking. Simmer the sauce very gently for
at least 30 minutes — but the longer the better. It can be left
in a very slow oven for a few hours. This sauce improves if it
is cooked the day before and reheated.
Serve the sauce very hot over spaghetti which has been
cooked in plenty of boiling, salted water, and drained. Top
with grated Parmesan cheese.

Wiener Schnitzel

Cooking time: 4-5 minutes

2 veal steaks
seasoned flour
1 egg, beaten
8-10 tablespoons dry breadcrumbs
4 oz butter
lemon wedges for garnish

Trim the veal into a neat shape and snip around the edge
with kitchen scissors, to prevent the Schnitzel from curling
up during frying. Beat veal lightly with a meat cleaver or
wooden rolling pin until 1/8-1/4 inch thin.
Place seasoned flour, beaten egg and dry breadcrumbs on
three individual plates.
Heat butter in a heavy frying pan.
Working quickly, dip the veal into the flour until coated
completely, then dip into the beaten egg, then into the
breadcrumbs. Press breadcrumbs on firmly with a knife and
put veal into the frying pan.
Fry quickly for 1-2 minutes until golden, turn over and fry
the other side 1-2 minutes. The perfect coating should
bubble in a few places.
Drain Schnitzel well on absorbent kitchen paper and serve at
once garnished with lemon wedges and accompanied with
potato salad and green salad.

Simple Cassoulet

Cooking time: 2¾ hours

12 oz stewing lamb chops, shoulder, or blade end
1 onion, sliced
1 tablespoon bacon fat
½ pint water or stock, made with stock cube
1 x 5 oz can tomato purée
6 oz dried haricot beans, soaked overnight
1 carrot, sliced
1 parsnip, sliced
1 stalk celery, sliced
sprig of parsley
pinch of dried thyme
1 bay leaf
freshly ground black pepper
salt

Sauté lamb, which has been previously trimmed and cut into
bite-sized pieces, and onion, in the heated fat in a heavy-based
pan until meat is lightly browned and onion is transparent.
Pour in a little water or stock then stir in the tomato purée.
Add the rest of the water or stock, the drained beans, carrot,
parsnip, celery, parsley, thyme, bay leaf and a grind of black
pepper.
Bring gently to the boil, cover and simmer gently until meat
is very tender, about 2 hours. Add salt to taste and simmer
gently for a further 30 minutes uncovered.
Serve hot.

Peasant Ragôut

Cooking time: 2-3 hours

1 lb stewing lamb chops, shoulder or blade end
2 lb large white onions, coarsely chopped
2 cloves garlic, crushed
2 tablespoons olive oil
1 pint red wine
1 x 5 oz can tomato purée
salt
freshly ground black pepper
1 bay leaf

Trim the lamb chops of all fat; leave bones in the chops as these may be easily removed later. Cut the meat into bite-sized pieces.
Fry the meat, onions and garlic in heated oil in a heavy-based pan until the onions are soft and the meat is lightly browned all over.
Add the remaining ingredients, cover and simmer as slowly as possible until the meat is very tender, about 2-3 hours.
This may also be cooked in a casserole in a very slow oven.
Remove the bones before serving.
Serve hot with boiled new potatoes or boiled rice.

Braised Garlic Lamb

Cooking time: 30 minutes

2 chump chops
2 tablespoons bacon fat
salt
freshly ground black pepper
8 cloves garlic, unpeeled
½ tablespoon plain flour
5 tablespoons stock, made with stock cube
1 tablespoon tomato purée

Fry the lamb chops lightly on both sides in the heated fat in a heavy-based frying pan. Add salt and pepper and place the garlic cloves (unpeeled) around the chops. Cook gently for 3 minutes.
Sprinkle the flour over the chops, add the stock and the tomato purée and simmer gently until the chops are tender. Add some more stock if necessary. Serve the lamb hot surrounded by the whole garlic cloves.

Stuffed Fillet of Beef

Oven temperature: 300-325° F, Gas Mark 1-3

Cooking time: 1½ hours

1 lb fillet of beef, in one piece
2 onions, sliced
beef dripping
2 anchovy fillets, chopped
1 tablespoon finely chopped bacon
pinch of pepper
pinch of dried thyme
pinch of finely chopped parsley
1 egg yolk

Trim the beef neatly.
Fry the sliced onions in about 1 tablespoon of dripping,
until they are golden brown.
Remove them from the pan, place in a mixing bowl and add
the anchovy fillets, bacon, pinch of pepper, thyme and.
parsley and the beaten egg yolk.
Cut the fillet in about four places, but not right through.
Put some of the stuffing into each cavity and tie the fillet up
with clean string or toothpicks.
Either wrap in greased foil and place in a roasting pan or
place in a covered roasting pan with a little dripping and cook
in a slow oven for 1½ hours or until tender.
Serve hot, cut into thick slices, accompanied by freshly
cooked vegetables.

Stuffed fillet of beef

Turkish Lamb Shanks

Cooking time: 3 hours

2 lamb shanks
plain flour
4 tablespoons olive oil
1 onion, chopped
1 clove garlic, crushed
1 green pepper, seeded, cored and chopped
1 teaspoon cumin seeds
1 teaspoon black peppercorns
1 x 15 oz can tomato juice
salt and pepper
juice of ½ lemon

Ask your butcher to chop through the bone in the lamb shanks.
Roll the shanks lightly in a little flour and brown lightly in the oil in a heavy-based pan. Add the onion and cook gently until the onion is soft.
Add the remaining ingredients, cover and simmer as slowly as possible until the meat is falling off the bone, at least 3 hours.
Serve hot, garnished with lemon wedges, accompanied with boiled brown rice.

Bocconcini

Cooking time: 15 minutes

4 small, very thin escalopes of veal
salt and pepper
2 rashers raw ham (or bacon), the same size as the veal
    escalopes
2 slices Gruyère cheese
1 egg
breadcrumbs for coating
3 oz butter
4 slices fried bread

54

Beat veal until 1/8 inch thick, trim into neat shapes and sprinkle with salt and pepper. On each piece of seasoned veal, place half a rasher of raw ham (or bacon) and half a slice of Gruyère cheese. Roll up veal and tie with string.
Coat each roll with beaten egg and breadcrumbs and fry in butter until golden and cooked. They are ready when the cheese is just melting.
Remove the string and serve on hot slices of fried bread.

Veal with Apples and Cream

Cooking time: 30 minutes

2 Granny Smith apples
2 escalopes of veal
salt and pepper
2 oz butter
1 shallot or spring onion, finely sliced
2 teaspoons brandy or Calvados
3 tablespoons cream

Peel and core the apples and cut into small cubes. Stew apples gently in a little water in a covered pan.
Season the veal with salt and pepper. Heat butter in a frying pan and just as it begins to turn brown, put in the veal and fry quickly for 2 minutes on each side, reduce heat and fry for 3 minutes on each side. Put aside and keep hot.
Fry the shallot in the pan, add the brandy and flame it.
Mash the cooked apples and add to the pan. Stir in the cream to make a smooth sauce. Season to taste with salt and pepper.
Pour the sauce over the escalopes and serve at once.

Lemon Garlic Kidneys

Cooking time: 5 minutes

6 lambs' kidneys
salt and pepper
1 clove garlic, chopped
1 tablespoon olive oil
juice of ½ lemon

Skin and core the kidneys and cut into ½ inch slices. Season with salt and pepper.
Fry the kidneys and garlic in hot oil quickly, moving them around all the time, for 3-4 minutes. Do not overcook.
Squeeze the lemon juice over the kidneys and remove from heat. Serve immediately on a bed of boiled white rice.

Garlic Chicken

Cooking time: 25 minutes

1½ oz butter
1 tablespoon olive oil
½ chicken jointed, or 2 chicken pieces
½ lemon
salt and pepper
10 plump, fresh cloves garlic, peeled but not crushed

Melt butter and oil in a heavy frying pan. Rub the chicken with the cut lemon and season with salt and pepper. Fry the garlic and chicken over a medium heat to seal in the juices but do not brown too fast. Turn from time to time. The chicken should cook in about 25 minutes.
Serve chicken hot with golden brown cloves of garlic and a crisp lettuce salad.

Shaslik

Cooking time: 15-20 minutes

12 oz lean chump chops
1 rasher bacon
6 tablespoons plain yoghurt
freshly ground black pepper
pinch each of dried thyme, rosemary and oregano
6 mushroom caps
2 tablespoons olive oil
¼ teaspoon salt
2 green peppers, seeded, cored and cut into 1½ inch squares
6 small whole tomatoes
6 bay leaves
6 small whole onions
juice of ½ lemon

Remove meat from chops, discard bones and fat and cut lamb
into 1½ inch cubes.
Rind bacon, remove any bones, cut into 1½ inch cubes.
Marinate the lamb in a mixture of yoghurt, pepper, thyme,
rosemary and oregano for at least 2 hours, turning at least
once. Marinate the mushroom caps in oil seasoned with salt.
Make sure that both sides of the mushroom caps are coated
with the oil.
Remove the lamb from the marinade and drain. Place pieces
of lamb on skewers, alternating lamb, green pepper, bacon,
mushroom caps, tomatoes, bay leaves and onions. Sprinkle
lightly with lemon juice and grill over hot charcoal or under
a hot grill.
Serve on a bed of parsley or shredded lettuce with wedges
of lemon.

Moussaka

Oven temperature: 350-375°, Gas Mark 4-5

Cooking time: 1½ hours

2 eggs (beaten)
½ pint milk
salt
freshly ground black pepper
1 large very ripe tomato, skinned and chopped
1 teaspoon sugar
1 clove garlic, crushed
1 tablespoon chopped onion
pinch of basil
olive oil for frying
2 onions, sliced
2 small aubergine, sliced but not peeled
12 oz leftover roast lamb or roast beef, finely minced
¼ pint stock, made with stock cube

This dish is delicious hot or cold and is an ideal way to use up
leftover lamb or beef.

Mix the beaten eggs with the milk, season with salt and pepper
and simmer gently until a thick custard forms. Put aside to
cool.
Make a tomato sauce by cooking together the tomato, sugar,
garlic, chopped onion and basil in a saucepan over a gentle
heat until most of the liquid has evaporated and you are left
with a very thick sauce. Mash with a wooden spoon and
season to taste with salt and pepper.
Fry the sliced onions and aubergine in oil until the onion is
golden and the aubergine is tender.
Grease the bottom and sides of a small rectangular cake or
loaf tin with a film of oil. Place alternate layers of the
aubergine mixture and minced meat in the tin. Pour in the
stock, cover with the tomato sauce and then spread the egg
mixture over the top. Cook in a moderate oven for 1 hour.
Turn out of the tin and serve hot or cold.

Chicken with Apricots

Cooking time: 30 minutes

½ large chicken
3 tablespoons oil
1 teaspoon plain flour
8 oz dried apricots, soaked overnight
approx. 1 pint apricot juice (from soaked fruit)
1 tablespoon chopped onion
1 teaspoon sugar
salt
pepper

Cut the chicken into bite-sized pieces and fry in oil in a
saucepan until golden. Remove from pan and keep warm.
Pour off all the oil except for 1 tablespoon. Stir the flour into
the oil and gradually add ½ pint of the liquid from the
soaked apricots, stirring continuously. Add the onion and
cook for another 5 minutes.
Return chicken pieces to the pan, add the sugar, salt and
pepper to taste, half the apricots and sufficient apricot juice
to cover the chicken well. Cover and simmer gently until the
chicken is tender.
Just before serving, add the remainder of the apricots and
apricot juice and reheat. Serve hot.
This dish improves if it is cooked the day before and
reheated.

Ratatouille with Eggs

Cooking time: 50 minutes

2 medium size potatoes
2 tomatoes
3 small courgettes
2 onions, peeled
1 red or green pepper, cored and seeded
4 tablespoons olive oil
2 cloves garlic, sliced
salt and pepper
2 eggs

Wash all the vegetables. Peel the potatoes, skin the tomatoes and cut the ends off the courgettes.
Slice all the vegetables into rounds.
Heat the oil in a heavy-based pan, add the vegetables and garlic and simmer, covered, for 30 minutes. Simmer for a further 20 minutes with the pan uncovered.
Season to taste with salt and pepper.
Serve ratatouille hot on individual dishes topped with a fried egg.

Curried Eggs

Cooking time: 30 minutes

8 oz onions, sliced
1 small red chilli, chopped
1 clove garlic, crushed
approx. ½ pint chicken stock, made with stock cube
½ teaspoon turmeric
1½ teaspoons curry powder
3 hard-boiled eggs
good pinch of salt

Combine onions, chilli, garlic, stock, turmeric and curry powder in a saucepan and simmer gently for 20-25 minutes.
Cut the eggs in half lengthways. Add the eggs and salt to the curry mixture and heat through gently.
Serve hot with boiled rice.

Turkish Poached Eggs

Cooking time: 5 minutes

¾ pint plain yoghurt
1 clove garlic, crushed
2 teaspoons white wine vinegar
salt
4 eggs
paprika pepper

Beat the yoghurt in a mixing bowl until smooth and stir in
the garlic, vinegar and salt to taste. Pour the mixture into two
individual serving dishes and top each with 2 poached eggs.
Melt the butter in a small pan, add just enough paprika to
colour it, season with salt to taste.
Pour melted butter mixture over the eggs and yoghurt and
serve immediately.
This may also be served cold.

Spiced Chicken

Cooking time: 20 minutes

½ chicken, jointed, or 2 chicken pieces
5 tablespoons plain yoghurt
1 teaspoon each ground cumin and coriander
¼ teaspoon ground cardamom
1 clove garlic, crushed
salt

Trim chicken into neat joints. Combine yoghurt, spices,
garlic and salt and cover the chicken completely with this
mixture. For the best results you should marinate the
chicken for several hours.
Grill chicken under a medium grill on pieces of aluminium
foil to retain the juices, for about 20 minutes or until cooked,
turning from time to time.
Serve hot with saffron rice.

Stuffed Picnic Loaf

Preparation time: 20 minutes

2 tomatoes, peeled and chopped
2 shallots or spring onions, chopped
1 green pepper, seeded, cored and chopped
8 black olives, stoned and chopped
1 tablespoon capers
1 dill pickled cucumber, chopped
1 small French loaf
olive oil
pinch of dried sweet basil
salt
freshly ground black pepper

This is ideal for a picnic and improves if made the day before.
Combine the tomatoes, shallots, green pepper, olives, capers
and dill pickled cucumber.
Cut the French loaf in half lengthways and scoop out all the
bread. Mix the crumbled bread with the tomato mixture, a
little olive oil, basil, salt and pepper.
Fill the two empty bread crust shells with the mixture, press
together, wrap the loaf securely in aluminium foil and chill.

Stuffed picnic loaf

Chicken Stew

Cooking time: 45 minutes

½ large chicken
juice of ½ lemon
pinch of ground cloves
¼ teaspoon ground cinnamon
1 teaspoon salt
¼ teaspoon pepper
5 tablespoons olive oil
3 tomatoes, skinned and chopped
1 tablespoon tomato puree
½ pint hot water

Cut the chicken into about four pieces. Mix together the
lemon juice, cloves, cinnamon, salt and pepper and rub into
the chicken.
Fry the chicken in the oil in a saucepan until golden brown.
Remove chicken from the pan and keep hot.
Put the tomatoes and tomato purée in the pan, stir into the
hot oil and add the hot water slowly. Simmer over a gentle
heat until the tomatoes have softened.
Return chicken to the pan, turn the pieces over a few times
to ensure they are covered with the sauce.
Cover and cook over a medium heat until the chicken is
tender. Serve hot.

Paprika Chicken

Cooking time: 30 minutes

1 onion, finely chopped
1½ oz butter
½ chicken
1 small tomato, skinned and finely chopped
salt
2 teaspoons paprika
2 tablespoons plain flour
2 tablespoons sour cream

Fry onion in heated butter in a saucepan until soft.
Cut the chicken into bite-sized pieces and add to the onion.
Add the tomato.
Stir in a pinch of salt and the paprika and gradually add
enough water to cover. Simmer, covered, until the chicken is
tender.
When the chicken is cooked, remove from the pan and keep
hot. Mix the sifted flour into the sour cream and slowly add
to the pan, stirring continuously. Bring gently to the boil,
stirring all the time, return chicken to the pan and reheat.
Serve hot with noodles.

Sesame Chicken

Cooking time: 15-20 minutes

2 chicken breasts, boned
2 oz butter, melted
1 tablespoon soy sauce
1 tablespoon white wine
½ teaspoon chopped tarragon
½ teaspoon mustard powder
sesame seeds

Prepare chicken breasts by removing bone with a sharp
filleting knife. Mix the butter, soy sauce, wine, tarragon and
mustard together. Marinate the chicken in this mixture for
3 hours. Drain and keep the marinade.
Grill the chicken for 4-6 minutes on each side. Remove from
heat, brush with the marinade, roll in sesame seeds and return
to heat until sesame seeds are golden brown.
Serve immediately.

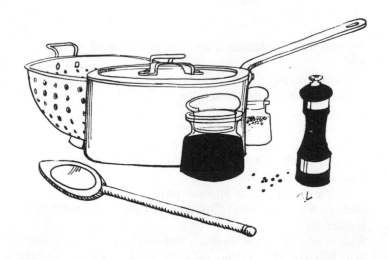

Chicken with Nut Sauce

Cooking time: 1¼ hours

½ boiled chicken
2 oz shelled walnuts
1 oz shelled almonds
1 oz shelled hazelnuts
paprika
salt
1 onion, chopped
1½ oz butter
¼ pint chicken stock

Cut the chicken into bite-sized pieces and keep hot.
Pound all the nuts together in a mortar with a pinch of
paprika and salt. Fry the chopped onion in the butter in a
saucepan for 5 minutes. Add the ground nuts and chicken
stock. Cover and simmer gently for 5 minutes.
Serve the chicken and sauce on boiled rice.

Cold Chicken with Sherry

Preparation time: 30 minutes

½ boiled chicken
1 egg yolk
¼ pint cream
2 tablespoons sherry
finely shredded lemon peel

This is a delicious way to use up leftover chicken.
Break or cut the chicken into bite-sized pieces, discard the
bones. Arrange in a serving bowl.
Beat the egg yolk with the cream and sherry. Cook, stirring
all the time, over a gentle heat until the sauce thickens
slightly. Pour sauce over the cold chicken and sprinkle with
lemon peel.
Serve chilled.

Mayonnaise

1 egg yolk
salt
olive oil, approx. ¼ pint
lemon juice

Whisk the egg yolk well with a pinch of salt, using a wooden
spoon. Continue stirring in the same direction all the time
and add the oil slowly, drop by drop, until the mayonnaise
is like a very thick custard. Add strained lemon juice drop by
drop, until the mayonnaise is to your taste.
Should the mixture curdle, put another beaten egg yolk into
a clean bowl and, using a clean spoon, gradually beat in the
curdled mayonnaise.
Variation: A tasty variation of mayonnaise is aioli, a garlic
mayonnaise which is very pleasant, if you're keen on garlic.
Serve it with plain, hot, boiled vegetables such as green beans,
small new potatoes, carrots and courgettes.
To make aioli: Prepare mayonnaise in the usual way, but add
4 finely chopped and pounded garlic cloves to the egg yolk
before adding the oil. Add plenty of finely chopped parsley
to the finished mayonnaise.

Egg Mayonnaise

Preparation time: 10-15 minutes

3 hard-boiled eggs
mayonnaise
chopped parsley

Pour a generous amount of good, home-made mayonnaise
into a shallow bowl and place the shelled, hard-boiled eggs,
cut in half lengthways, on it, cut side down. Sprinkle with
a little finely chopped parsley. Serve slightly chilled with
salad.

Salads and Vegetables

Niçoise Salad

Preparation time: 15 minutes

½ small lettuce, washed and cut into 4 wedges
1 hard-boiled egg, halved
1 very firm small tomato, cut into segments
4 anchovy fillets
4 black olives
4 capers
¼ red or green pepper, cored, seeded and sliced
3 tablespoons olive oil
1 tablespoon tarragon vinegar
1 clove garlic, crushed
1 tablespoon chopped fresh basil
salt and freshly ground black pepper

Arrange all the ingredients, except for the oil, vinegar, garlic, basil, salt and pepper, on a serving plate (not in a dish or salad bowl) and chill until ready to serve.
Just before serving, pour a dressing — made by shaking the remaining ingredients (except for the basil) together in a screw-top jar — over the salad. The basil is then lightly sprinkled over the finished salad.

Tomato and Rice Salad

Preparation time: 25 minutes

4 oz uncooked white rice
salt
1 slice lemon
2 tablespoons olive oil
2 teaspoons tarragon vinegar
pinch of ground nutmeg
2 large ripe tomatoes, skinned and sliced
chopped parsley for garnish

Cook the rice in plenty of boiling, salted water with a slice of lemon until tender. Drain the rice, discard the lemon, and immediately stir in the olive oil, vinegar, a pinch of salt and nutmeg.
Put in a serving bowl and arrange the tomato on top of the rice and sprinkle with parsley. Chill before serving.

Spinach Salad

Preparation time: 10 minutes

8 oz spinach
2 cold, boiled potatoes, thinly sliced
3 slices Gruyere cheese, cut into strips
1 tablespoon cream
juice of ¼ lemon
salt
freshly ground black pepper

Cut spinach leaves from stem and wash well.
Cook the spinach in a covered saucepan for 3 minutes.
Drain spinach well and mix with the cold potatoes, cheese, cream, lemon juice and salt and pepper to taste.
Serve hot or cold.

Orange Mint Salad

Preparation time: 10 minutes

2 sweet, thin-skinned navel oranges
1 tablespoon finely chopped mint
3 tablespoons olive oil
2 teaspoons lemon juice
2 teaspoons Cognac

Peel the oranges with a serrated knife and neatly remove all
the white pith.
Slice oranges and discard ends. Arrange slices overlapping on
a serving plate and sprinkle with mint.
Combine oil, lemon juice and Cognac in a screw-top jar,
shake well and pour over the oranges. Chill before serving.

Green Bean Salad

Preparation time: 10 minutes

8 oz green beans, preferably the thin, stringless variety
salt
1 clove garlic, cut in half
2 tablespoons olive oil
2 teaspoons lemon juice
freshly ground black pepper

Wash the beans and cut into 2 inch pieces. Cook in boiling,
salted water until just tender.
Drain the beans and place in a salad bowl which has been
previously rubbed with the garlic. Sprinkle with oil and
lemon juice. Season with black pepper, taste and add salt if
necessary. Chill before serving.

Sweet and Sour Cabbage

Oven temperature: 300-325° F, Gas Mark 1-3

Cooking time: 2 hours

¼-½ small red cabbage
1 green cooking apple, peeled, cored and thinly sliced
1 onion, thinly sliced
salt
freshly ground black pepper
1 tablespoon sugar
1 sprig of parsley
1 bay leaf
pinch of thyme
1 tablespoon port wine
1 tablespoon wine vinegar

A very nice accompaniment to pork.
Remove the tough outside leaves of the cabbage, cut out the
stalk and cut the cabbage into segments. Slice thinly.
Place the cabbage in a casserole in alternate layers with apple
and onion. Season each layer with salt and pepper and sugar.
Put the herbs in the middle layer.
Pour the port and vinegar over and cook, covered, in a slow
oven for about 2 hours. Serve hot.

Coleslaw

Preparation time: 10 minutes

8 oz thinly shredded cabbage (about ¼ small cabbage)
2 tablespoons olive oil
1 tablespoon white vinegar
½ teaspoon sugar
½ red apple, cored and chopped but not peeled
1 tablespoon raisins

Combine all the ingredients well and chill, covered, for several
hours before serving.
Stir the coleslaw occasionally while it is in the refrigerator.

Vegetable Casserole

Cooking time: 30 minutes

2 green peppers
8 oz green beans, stringed
2 onions, peeled and chopped
1 clove garlic, crushed
¼ pint olive oil
1 ripe tomato, skinned and chopped
8 oz potatoes, peeled and chopped
freshly ground black pepper
sour cream or yoghurt for serving

Cut the tops from the green peppers, discard white cores and
seeds. Cut peppers into rounds about ¼ inch wide. Cut beans
in half.
Fry the onions and garlic in the oil in a heavy-based pan or
flameproof casserole until transparent. Add tomato, beans,
green pepper and potatoes. Add pepper to taste. Cover with
a very tight lid, bring to the boil quickly, then reduce heat
and simmer slowly until the vegetables are quite soft.
Serve hot, topped with sour cream or yoghurt.

Carrots Vichy

Cooking time: 10-15 minutes

8-12 oz small new carrots
1 oz butter
pinch of salt
2 teaspoons sugar
¾ pint water
chopped parsley for garnish

Scrape the carrots, wash and dry well and cut into ¼ inch
thick rounds.
Cook in a small heavy-based pan with ½ oz butter, salt, sugar
and water.
Cook with the saucepan uncovered, until the carrots are
tender and almost all the water has evaporated. If there is any
water left in the pan, drain it off. Add the rest of the butter
and shake the pan to prevent the carrots sticking.
Serve immediately, garnished with finely chopped parsley.

Mushrooms in Cream Sauce

Cooking time: 7 minutes

8 oz mushrooms
1 oz butter
1 tablespoon olive oil
pinch of salt
freshly ground black pepper
pinch of nutmeg
1 tablespoon finely chopped parsley
½ shallot finely chopped
4 tablespoons thick cream

Wipe mushrooms clean with a clean, damp cloth, slice thinly.
Heat butter and oil in a frying pan and cook mushrooms over
a medium heat for 1 minute then add salt, pepper, nutmeg,
parsley and shallot. Stir the mushrooms occasionally to
prevent them from sticking to the pan.
Stir in the cream and continue cooking gently for 5 minutes.
Serve immediately.

Potatoes Dauphinois

Oven temperature: 300-325° F, Gas Mark 1-3

Cooking time: 1½ hours

1½ lb potatoes
1 clove garlic, crushed
salt and pepper
½ pint cream
1 oz butter

Peel the potatoes and slice into thin rounds. Wash them in
cold water and dry lightly in a clean tea towel.
Arrange in layers in a greased shallow ovenproof dish,
previously rubbed with the garlic. Season to taste with salt
and pepper.
Pour the cream over and dot with butter. Bake for about 1½
hours in a slow oven.
To obtain a crust on top of the potatoes, turn the oven up to
high for the last 10 minutes. Serve hot.

Desserts

Melon and Grapes

Preparation time: 10 minutes

1 small melon (honeydew, cantaloup or rockmelon)
1 tablespoon castor sugar
1 lemon
1 small bunch seedless grapes

Remove skin and seeds carefully from melon and cut melon flesh into cubes.
Place in a serving bowl, sprinkle with sugar and squeeze lemon juice over. Add washed, slightly crushed grapes. Serve chilled.

Pears in Red Wine

Cooking time: 30 minutes

2 fresh, firm pears
red wine
1 clove
1 small stick of cinnamon, crushed
4 oz sugar
1 tablespoon brandy or Cognac

Peel the pears carefully, leaving the stalks on. Place the pears in a deep saucepan, just wide enough to accommodate them. Pour in enough red wine to cover, add the clove, cinnamon stick and sugar, cover and cook over a low heat until the pears are tender.
Carefully remove the pears and serve with some of the liquor plus the brandy or Cognac poured over.
Serve hot or cold.

80   Melon and grapes

Pineapple with Kirsch

Preparation time: 5 minutes

½ small ripe pineapple
castor sugar
1 tablespoon Kirsch

Peel and core the pineapple, cut into ½ inch slices and then
into bite-sized pieces.
Arrange on a flat round dish, sprinkle with sugar and Kirsch,
and serve.

Strawberry Whip

Preparation time: 10 minutes

1 punnet strawberries
¼ pint cream
1 egg white
1 tablespoon castor sugar

Clean and hull the strawberries, put aside six good ones for
decoration, and mash the rest to a pulp.
Whip the cream, fold in the stiffly whisked egg white, then
the strawberries. Stir in the sugar.
Pile mixture into individual goblets or glass bowls and
decorate with the whole strawberries.

Bananas with Kirsch and Cream

Preparation time: 5 minutes

2 large ripe bananas
castor sugar
2 teaspoons Kirsch
2 tablespoons cream

Peel and slice the bananas, sprinkle with sugar and Kirsch and stir in the cream. Mix gently, but thoroughly, to ensure that the banana is properly coated with the mixture. Serve at room temperature.

Fried Bananas with Rum

Cooking time: 5 minutes

2 large bananas
1 oz butter
juice of ¼ lemon
2 tablespoons rum
castor sugar

Peel the bananas and cut in half lengthways. Melt the butter in a frying pan and as it begins to bubble, put in the bananas. Cook them very gently on both sides for 2 minutes, add the lemon juice. Flame with rum (warm it in a ladle or spoon, ignite and pour over the bananas).
Sprinkle with sugar and serve immediately. Delicious with cream.
Variation: Use brandy in place of rum, or a mixture of rum and brandy.

Peaches in Wine

Preparation time: 5 minutes

2 large, ripe, unblemished peaches
castor sugar
lemon juice
red wine or chilled white dessert wine

Peel peaches carefully and slice into two goblets.
Sprinkle the peaches with plenty of sugar and a little lemon
juice. Just before serving, pour enough wine into the goblets
to just reach the top of the fruit. Serve immediately.
Try using a rosé wine or Champagne or Sauterne.

Pears in Cream

Oven temperature: 350-375° F, Gas Mark 4-5

Cooking time: 15-30 minutes.

2 firm but ripe pears
½ oz butter
2 tablespoons vanilla sugar
3 tablespoons cream

Peel, quarter, core and slice the pears.
Melt the butter in a shallow flameproof dish, big enough to
take all the pears in one layer. Add the pears and sugar and
cook very gently over a low heat until the pears are tender
(anything from 10-25 minutes, depending on how ripe the
pears are).
Stir in the cream and cook for 2 minutes, shaking the pan
occasionally.
Place in a moderate oven for 5 minutes. Serve hot.
Note: For vanilla sugar, see page 88.

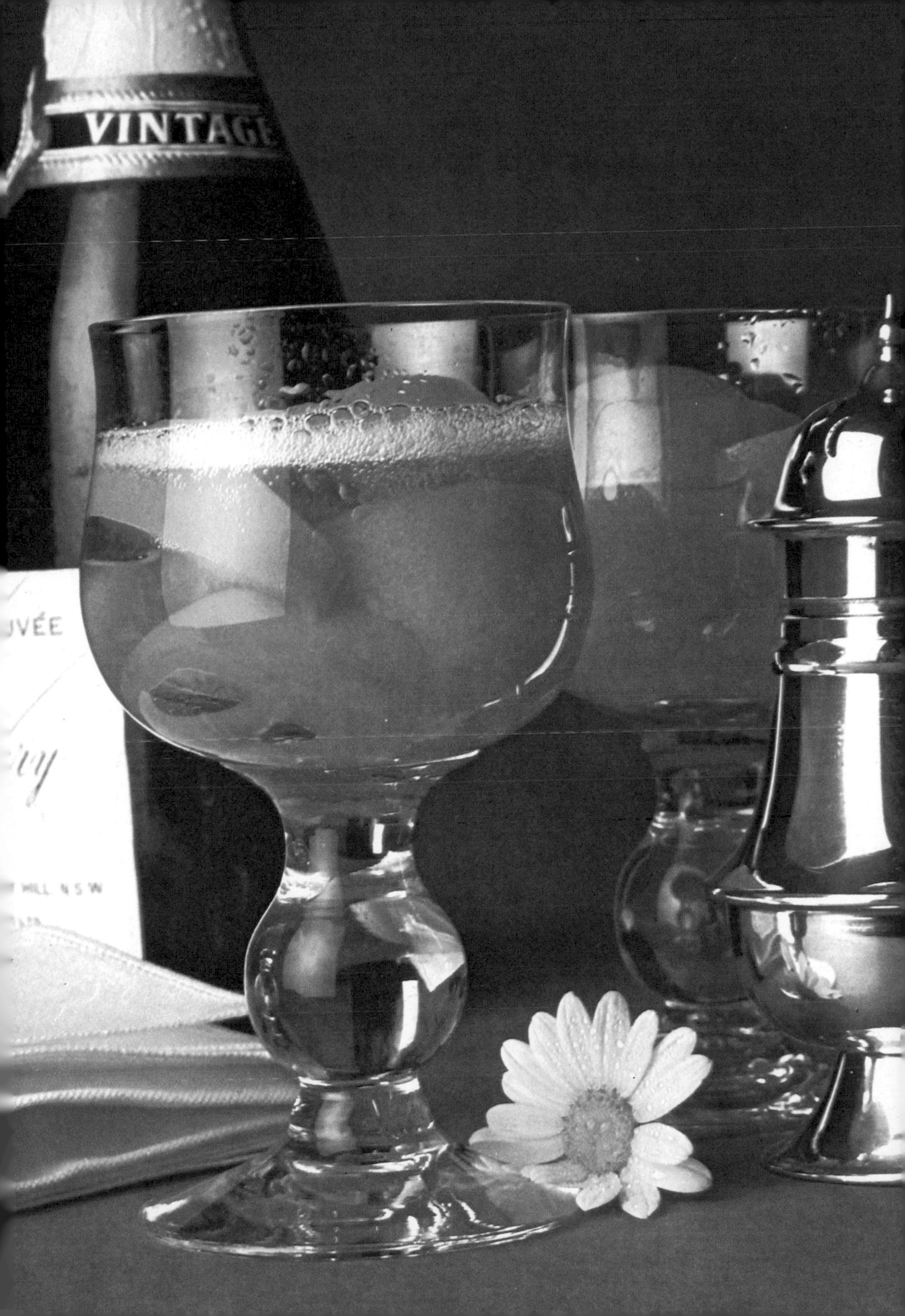
VINTAGE

Rich Egg Custard

Oven temperature: 300-325° F, Gas Mark 1-3

Cooking time: 45 minutes

2 eggs
1½ tablespoons sugar
½ pint milk
ground nutmeg

Beat the eggs, sugar and milk well. Pour into a small buttered
ovenproof dish and sprinkle lightly with nutmeg.
Place in a baking dish filled with enough cold water to come
half way up the sides of the ovenproof dish and bake
uncovered in a slow oven until custard is set, about 45
minutes. Serve hot or cold with canned or stewed fruit.
If serving hot, leave to cool slightly for 10 minutes.

Steamed Sultana Pudding

Cooking time: 1 — 1½ hours

4 oz butter
4 oz (½ cup) castor sugar
1 large egg
2 oz (½ cup) self raising flour, sifted
½ teaspoon mixed spice
6 oz (1 cup) sultanas
1 tablespoon chopped walnuts
4 tablespoons milk

Cream butter and sugar in a mixing bowl, until light in
colour and fluffy in texture.
Beat in beaten egg in two stages.
Fold in sifted flour and spices.
Gently mix in sultanas, walnuts and milk.
Put mixture into a small, greased pudding basin. Cover
tightly with a layer of greased, greaseproof paper and
aluminium foil and steam over rapidly boiling water for
1-1½ hours, or until an inserted skewer will come out clean.
Serve hot with cream or custard sauce.

Wholemeal Honey Cakes

Makes 8 — 12

Oven temperature: 400-450°F.

Cooking time: 20 minutes

8 oz fine wholemeal flour
½ teaspoon salt
3 teaspoons baking powder
½ teaspoon ground cinnamon
½ teaspoon ground nutmeg
3 oz butter
1 tablespoon sultanas
1 tablespoon chopped walnuts
4 tablespoons honey
milk to mix if necessary

Sift wholemeal flour, salt, baking powder and spices
into a mixing bowl.
Rub butter into flour until mixture resembles breadcrumbs.
Stir in sultanas, walnuts, warmed honey and sufficient milk
to mix to a stiff dough.
Turn dough out onto a lightly floured board and roll out
to ½ inch thick. Cut into 2 inch rounds with a scone cutter
and place on a lightly floured baking tray.
Bake in a hot oven for 20 minutes.
Serve warm spread with butter and honey.

Berry Mould

Preparation time: 45 minutes

½ punnet strawberries
8 oz fresh black cherries, stoned
1 green cooking apple, peeled, cored and sliced
4 oz sugar
sliced white bread or sliced raisin loaf
cream for serving.

Put the cleaned fruit in a pan with the sugar (use more or
less depending on how sweet the fruit is). Cover and heat
very gently until the juice leaves the fruit, stirring constantly
to prevent the fruit from sticking. Crush the fruit slightly
with a wooden spoon.
Grease the inside of a small pudding bowl and line with thin
slices of crustless bread or raisin loaf. Fill with the fruit and
top with more bread or raisin loaf.
Grease the bottom of a small plate or saucer that will fit into
the top of the bowl, place it on top of the pudding and put
a weight on top of this. Chill overnight. Turn out and serve
with cream.

Apples with Calvados

Cooking time: 10 minutes

3 Granny Smith apples
1½ oz butter
2 tablespoons vanilla sugar
2 tablespoons Calvados

Peel apples, cut into quarter segments, remove core and slice
thinly. Gently cook the apples in the melted butter, along
with the sugar, in a frying pan until pale golden and
transparent. When turning the apple slices, do so gently to
avoid breaking them.
When apples are tender, flame with the Calvados (warm it
over a flame in a soup ladle or spoon, ignite and pour over
apples). When the flames go out, serve apples immediately.
Note: Vanilla sugar is castor sugar which is flavoured with a
vanilla bean. You may make it yourself by placing a vanilla
bean in a jar of castor sugar or you may buy it from leading
grocery departments.

Berry mould

Chocolate Semolina

Cooking time: 20-25 minutes
Oven temperature: 350-375° F.

½ pint milk
1 tablespoon cocoa
2 tablespoons sugar
2 tablespoons semolina
3 drops vanilla essence
1 oz butter
1 egg

Mix a little of the measured milk in a small bowl with the cocoa and sugar, to form a smooth paste.
Bring remainder of milk to boil in a saucepan. Sprinkle in semolina and cocoa mixture and bring to the boil, stirring continuously.
Simmer over a low heat for 1-2 minutes.
Remove from heat and stir in vanilla, butter and beaten egg.
Pour into a small, greased pie dish and bake in a moderate oven (350-375°F.) for 20-25 minutes.
Serve hot with pouring cream if desired.

Superman Special

Cooking time: 40-45 minutes

Oven temperature: 350-375° F.

½ pint milk
1 tablespoon castor sugar
1 oz butter
1 cup cake crumbs
1 egg
3 drops vanilla essence
2 tablespoons sultanas

Place milk in a saucepan with sugar and butter and bring just to the boil.
Cook for 5 minutes then stir in cake crumbs.

Beat egg, add vanilla and stir into basic mixture along with sultanas.
Pour into two individual greased ovenproof dishes or a small pie dish and place in a baking dish. Pour in water to cover half way up pudding dishes.
Bake in a moderate oven for 40-45 minutes.
Serve hot or cold.

Country Junket

Preparation time: ¾ — 1¼ hours

1 pint fresh milk
2 junket tablets or 1 tablespoon rennet
1 tablespoon castor sugar
1 tablespoon rum
¼ teaspoon ground nutmeg
¼ teaspoon ground cinnamon
strawberry jam and whipped cream for serving

Make junket with lukewarm milk and junket tablets, according to directions on bottle.
Stir in sugar, rum and spices and pour into a warm bowl.
Leave to set at room temperature, ½ — 1 hour.
Serve topped with strawberry jam and whipped cream.

Cream Trifle

Preparation time: 1¼ hours

¼ pint thick (double) cream
1 tablespoon golden syrup
2 tablespoons rum
2 sponge fingers
sliced strawberries or Chinese gooseberries for decoration
juice of 1 small lemon

Pour cream into a small mixing bowl and mix in warmed golden syrup and rum.
Slice sponge fingers and place in the bottom of two individual serving bowls.
Pour cream mixture over and cover with sliced fruit.
Chill for 1 hour.
Sprinkle lemon juice over just before serving.

Index

93